Toddler Coloring Book
Fruits and Vegetables

Persimmon

Broccoli

Cherry

Garlic

Apple

Pea

Cauliflower

Lemon

Apple

Orange

Strawberry

Kiwi

Cherry

Grape

Rose apple

Pineapple

Avocado

Watermelon

Banana

Lemon

Persimmon

Peach

Papaya

Mango

Melon

Blackberry

Dragonfruit

Mangosteen

Chiness pear

Rambutan

Guava

Fig

Durian

Custard apple

Pomelo

Tamarind

Blueberry

Rasberry

Pumpkin

Tomato

Carrot

Potato

Leek

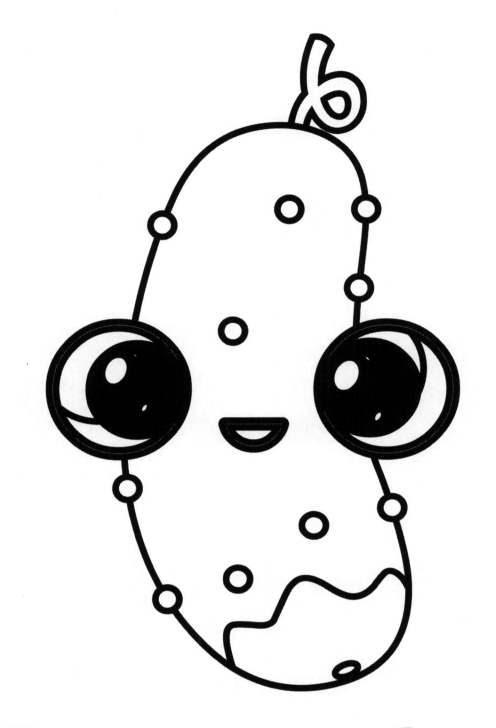

Cucumber

Onion

Corn

Cabbage

Mushroom

Garlic

Chile pepper

Broccoli

Bell pepper

Beetroot

Eggplant

Pea

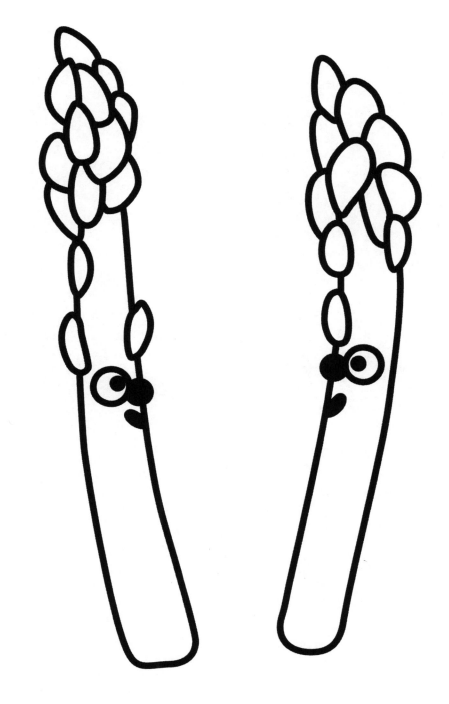

Asparagus

Radish

Chinese cabbage

Cauliflower

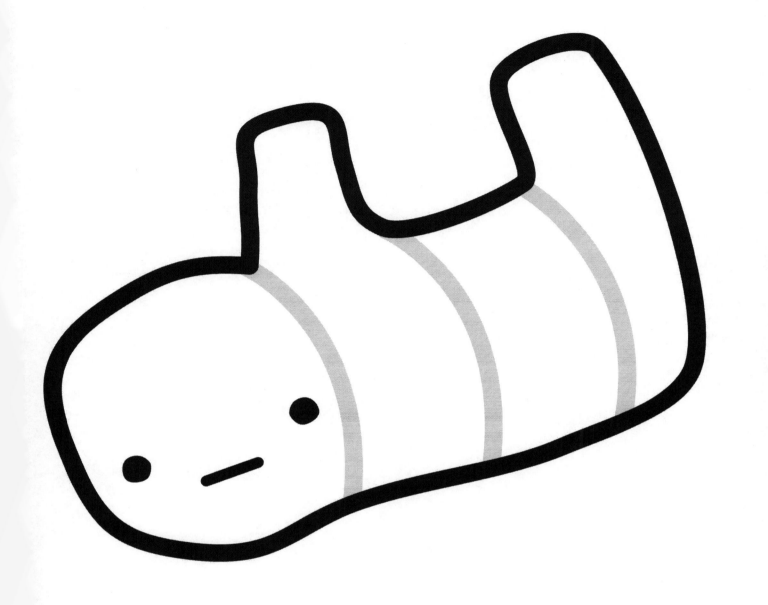

Ginger

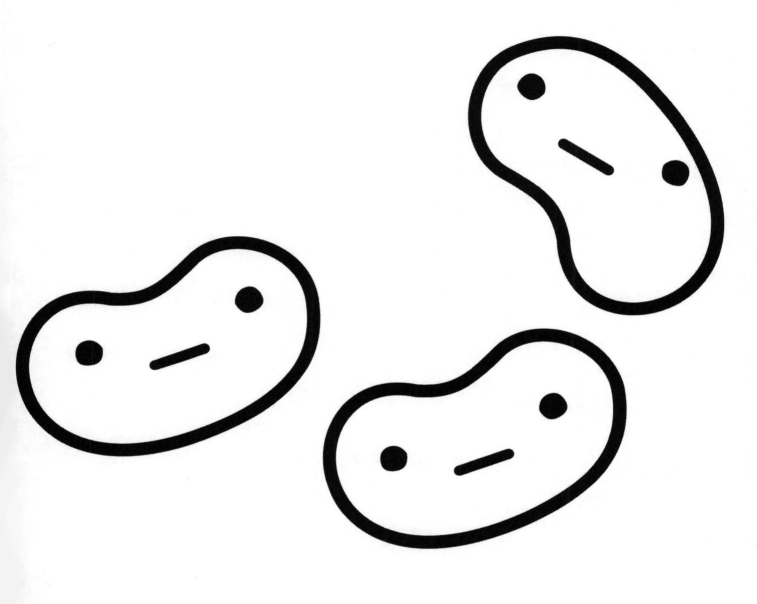

Beans

red cabbage

Winter melon

90391480R00064

Made in the USA
San Bernardino, CA
09 October 2018